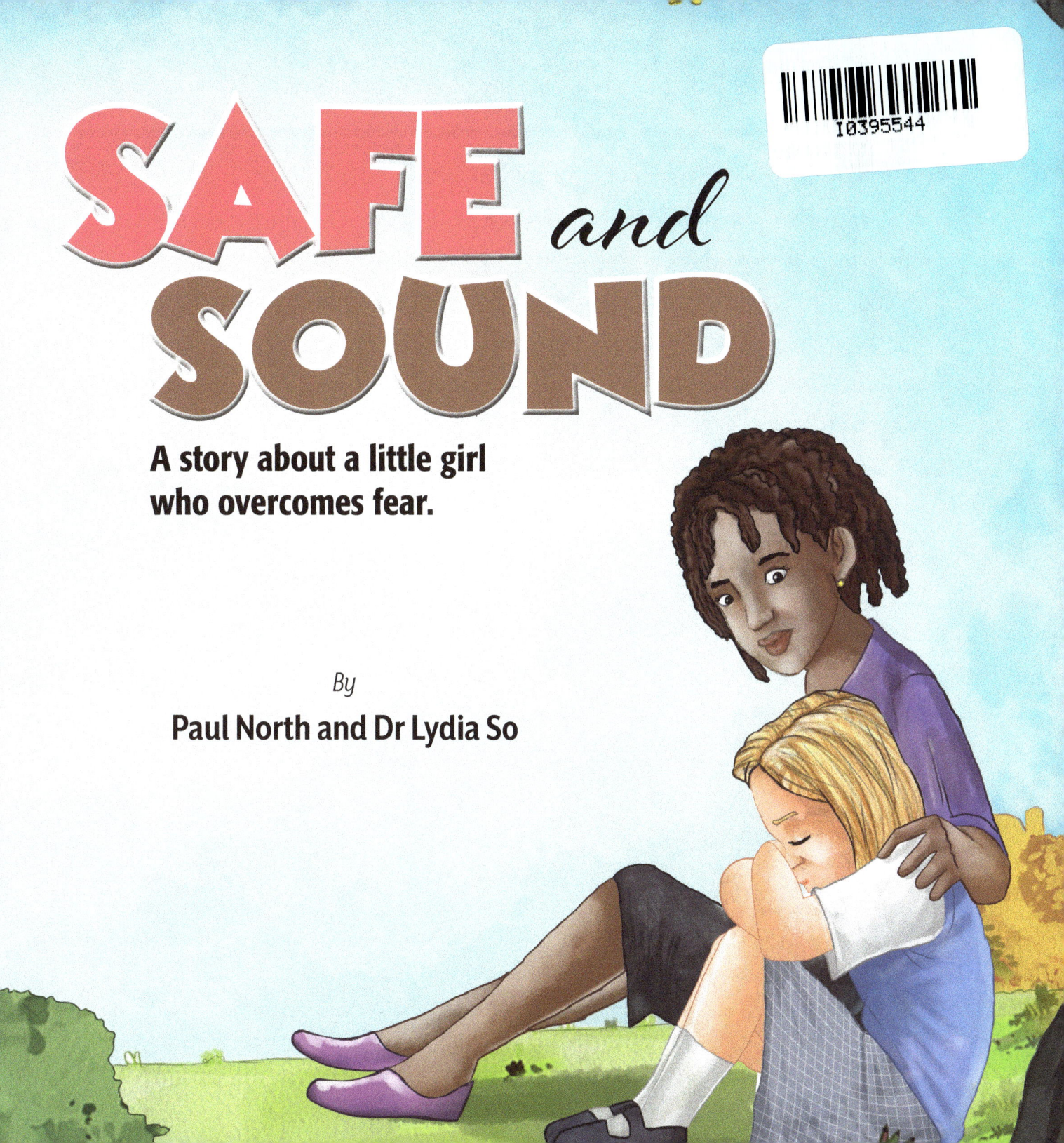

SAFE and SOUND

A story about a little girl who overcomes fear.

By
Paul North and Dr Lydia So

The following story is based upon the brilliant work of arguably the world's leading neuroscientist, Dr Stephen Porges. Dr Porges is renowned for the development of the Polyvagal Theory, a breakthrough description in understanding how our autonomic nervous system drives our emotional and cognitive states. Polyvagal Theory teaches that all behaviour is the person's best attempt to adapt to threat (perceived or real) in their life. The greatest gift we can give any person, even ourselves, is the gift of safety. Then we are ready to take on the world...

 A catalogue record for this book is available from the National Library of Australia

Copyright © 2020 PNorth and LSO.

All rights reserved. No part of this publication may be reproduced, stored in a retrieval system, or transmitted in any form or by any means, electronic, mechanical, photocopying, recording or otherwise without prior permission of the author.

Publisher:
Inspiring Publishers
P.O. Box 159, Calwell, ACT Australia 2905
Email: publishaspg@gmail.com
http://www.inspiringpublishers.com

National Library of Australia Cataloguing-in-Publication entry

Author: Paul North and Dr Lydia So

Title: **SAFE and SOUND:** *A story about a little girl who overcomes fear*/Paul North and Dr Lydia So

ISBN: 978-1-922327-24-6 (print)
978-1-922327-27-7 (eBook)

Dedication

To every child who gets scared by loud noises, stormy nights and scary thoughts. You hold the keys to a better world.

CRACK went the thunder!
Poor Chloe curled up even tighter in her bed. She tried to call out to her Dad for help, but her voice didn't work.

All that came out was a tiny squeak.

She shivered, but she wasn't cold.
Her body wouldn't work properly.
Chloe wondered if she was even there…
That was until the next flash of lightning filled the room with light and shadows.

Suddenly, her body came back to life.
She jumped out of her bed, feet barely touching
the ground. Chloe ran across the bedroom
and straight into her Dad's warm embrace.

Dad said, "You're safe now Chloe,
it's going to be OK."
He sung Chloe her favourite lullaby.

Cradling her, carrying her,
Chloe felt normal again.
The big storm was still scary,
but it was outside. Inside, in her father's
protective embrace she was safe and sound.
When she felt safe, her body worked.

Chloe's body didn't always work the way she wanted it to. Sometimes it let her down. Sometimes she felt all shaky.

Even when she didn't want to feel shaky. Like the time she had to recite her times tables in front of the class. But when Chloe stood up, her body started to tremble. Her voice didn't work properly. Her brain felt foggy. Then two girls laughed at her.

Chloe just froze.

Chloe's teacher, Mrs Burke kept calling her name, "Chloe, Chloe, Chloe."

Suddenly Chloe exploded.

She called the two girls rude names and then she ran out of the classroom.

Mrs Burke found Chloe sitting under a tree, crying. She put her arm around her. Chloe looked into Mrs Burke's friendly eyes and asked, "Why do I get so scared?"

Mrs Burke wasn't sure, but she said she would help Chloe to find out. Mrs Burke called Chloe's parents and she suggested that Chloe see a doctor who specialised in helping children.

Chloe's parents took her to see Dr Lydia, a Paediatrician who listened to Chloe's story.

Dr Lydia examined Chloe and said she had previously had a kind of ear infection called Otitis Media. A funny name for a blocked-up ear. She suggested that Chloe have a hearing test.

Dr Lydia also suggested that Chloe see a psychologist. She told Chloe that it wasn't her fault that she was feeling scared or angry, because it was her body trying to protect her from scary situations.

Chloe felt better when she heard that. Most of the grown-ups she had met had told her she was naughty and needed to be better behaved.

The psychologist's name was Mr North.
He figured out that Chloe was very good
at hearing low sounds like trucks, air-conditioners
and trains. This was because the ear infections
made Chloe's ears better at hearing scary sounds
than hearing soothing, happy sounds.

He also guessed that Chloe would be afraid of big noises like barking dogs and slamming doors. He was right.

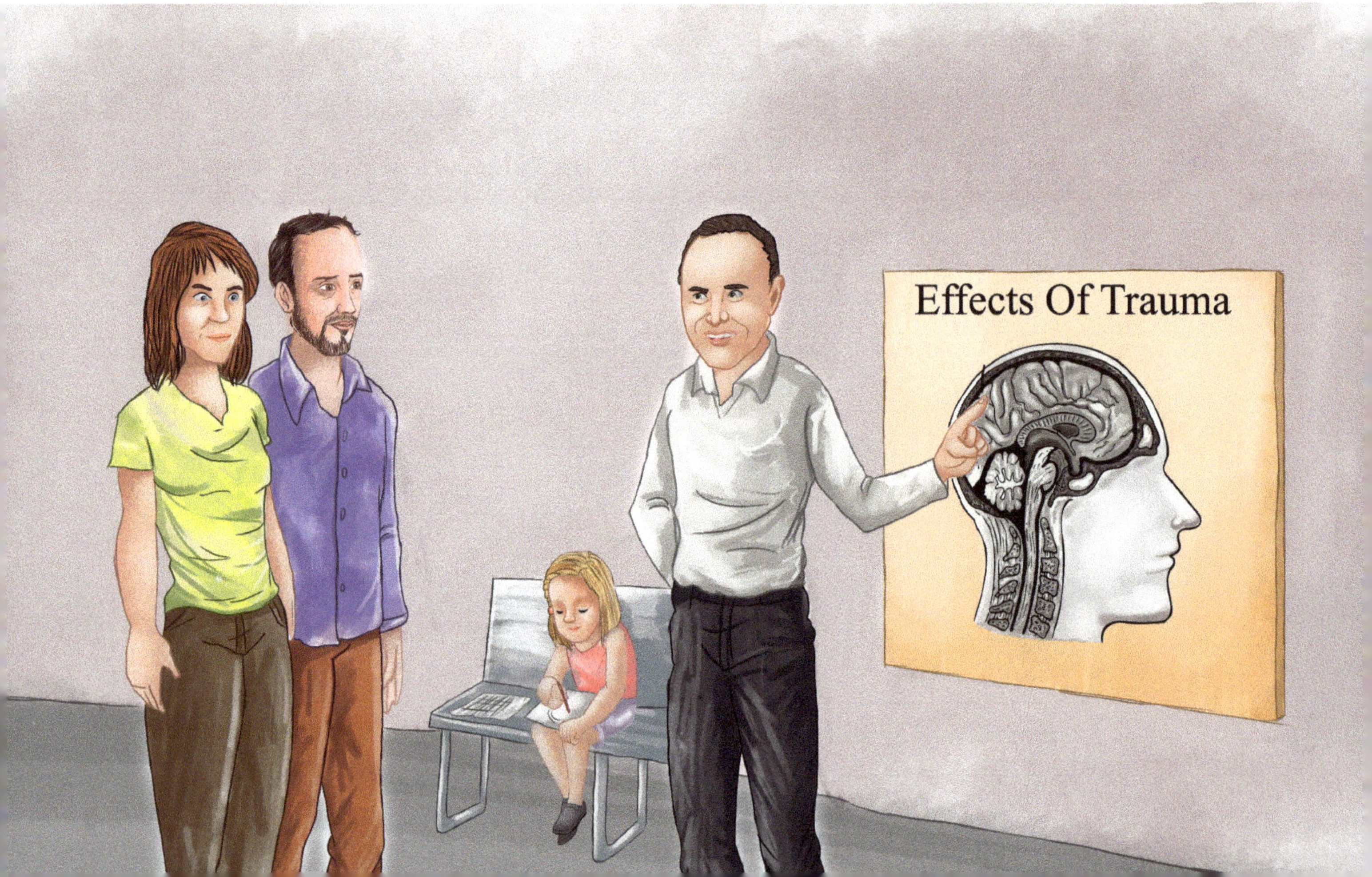

Effects Of Trauma

Mr North said if scary things happen
when a person is younger,
changes can occur in the brain and body
that affect their behaviour.

Mr North said that Chloe's body was always trying to feel safe, but that sometimes what her body did got her into trouble…

Mr North said he would help Chloe be in control of feeling safe.

Mr North found out that Chloe had experienced some scary things when she was younger.

Three years ago, Chloe's Dad lost his job. He became sad and angry.

When Chloe looked at her Dad's face back then, she also felt sad and scared.

She didn't know what to say to make him feel better. She was afraid to approach him.

She stayed quiet in her room and felt very alone. Sometimes she cried and couldn't help it.

Then Mum and Dad started fighting.
Dad would drink too much beer,
slam the doors and pound his fist
on the table. That would make Chloe
jump and her heart beat faster.

As time went by, Chloe found herself jumping at other loud sounds, such as a motorbike going past in the street. Sometimes she even got in trouble for being startled at school, and that made her feel worse.

Then things got better.
Dad got another job and
Mum and Dad saw a counsellor.

At the next visit, Mr North taught Chloe how to breathe in a special way using feedback from a computer game.

Deep, slow, even breathing helped Chloe feel calmer and do well at the game.

Another breathing exercise involved having a short breathe in, followed by a long breathe out, like when someone blows bubbles.

Chloe was so clever that she invented a game where she and her mum would see how far down the hallway they could blow a bubble.

Mum and Chloe loved that game.
The breathing helped Mum feel calm too.
Mr North said that if Chloe practiced blowing bubbles every day, her body would start to feel safe. He was right, after a short while Chloe's body felt safer and she felt happier.

Mum and Dad asked
Mr North if they should get a cat for Chloe,
he thought that was great idea.

Chloe named her cat Toby and they became best friends.

Chloe worried about the future a lot and felt bad about things in the past.

To fix this, Mr North taught Chloe about the present moment. During one session, Chloe had to count Toby's breaths by watching his tummy move up and down. When Chloe did this, she began to feel calm.

Over the following sessions, Mr North had Chloe listen to some special music through headphones. It was kind of fun and Chloe coloured in whilst she listened and sang along.

Sometimes the music was a little quiet and sometimes it sounded a little weird, but it helped Chloe's hearing become more settled.

A few days after finishing her treatment, Chloe's Mum and Dad started to notice positive changes.

Chloe was brave now.

Not long after Chloe's seventh birthday,
a big storm started to brew on the horizon.
Chloe raced to the window and watched
it come in. Instead of being scared,
she was wide eyed and curious.

CRACK went the thunder!

Poor Toby ran and hid inside
Chloe's dressing gown.

"It's going to be OK Toby, you're safe now," said Chloe as she sang Toby a lullaby and stroked his head.

In the doorway, Mum and Dad watched their little girl, with Toby curled up in her lap. She was no longer concerned about the storm in the background. Both Chloe and Toby were safe and sound now.

Thanks to Dr Lydia and Mr North, Chloe and her family learnt why it's so important to feel safe. With practice and over time, you can feel safe too.

About the Authors:

Paul North is an Australian psychologist with over 30 years of experience in the field of developmental disabilities and trauma therapy, assisting both children and adults. He has worked at the most senior levels of Government in both New South Wales and the Australian Capital Territory as both a clinician and consultant.

Dr Lydia So is a New Zealand born Developmental Paediatrician, now working in Australia as a Staff Specialist based in a suburban Sydney hospital. She also has a private practice in Canberra where she assists children with a range of developmental disabilities, including Autism Spectrum Disorder.

Parents and Teachers:

For more information regarding the scientific background to this book, visit www.partnershipsplus.com.au *and see the section on Safe and Sound.*

For information concerning how to understand trauma and the role of the body in adapting to that trauma please visit the following sites:

https://www.stephenporges.com
https://integratedlistening.com
https://unyte.com
https://www.heartmath.com
https://monadelahooke.com

Resources:

Stephen W. Porges, The Pocket Guide to Polyvagal Theory: The Transformative Power of Feeling Safe (New York: W.W. Norton, 2017).

Mona Delahooke, Beyond Behaviors (PESI, 2019).